MANIFEST AND MASTER YOUR TALENT

Overcome Self-Doubt, Elevate Your Mindset, Cultivate Your Skills, and Achieve Lasting Success

By

PREM PRAKASH DUTTA

Email:  Connect2prem2020@outlook.com

★ ★ ★

PREFACE

Wisdom has been shared with humanity in countless ways—through books, paintings, stories, and even the smallest moments of life. The form doesn't matter; what matters is how we receive and apply it.

We hold pieces of this wisdom scattered across time and cultures. Some recognize these fragments, collecting them like treasures, while others pass them by without a second thought. Those who gather and embrace more of this knowledge shape lives filled with depth, purpose, and meaning.

This book is an invitation to see those fragments more clearly, to connect the dots that lead to a richer understanding of talent, growth, and the extraordinary potential within us. What you take from these pages is up to you. But one thing is certain—the more wisdom you gather, the more vibrant and fulfilling your life becomes.

Let's begin.

Acknowledgment

I am deeply grateful to my mentor, Som Batla sir, whose guidance and unwavering support gave me the strength to complete this book. His wisdom has been a constant source of inspiration.

I also thank my parents, who have always believed in me—no matter what path I chose or what dreams I pursued, they stood by my side with endless encouragement and blessings. Their faith in me has been my greatest motivation.

This book reflects the support, belief, and wisdom I've received. To all who have been part of this journey—thank you.

TABLE OF CONTENTS

Chapter 1

Introduction

Over the centuries, many thinkers and philosophers have had different views on talent. Some suggest it is just a skill that develops over time in an individual in a particular environment. In contrast, some strongly argue that talent is an innate ability to do certain things way better than others. Talent can be gained from practice and innate, although innate talent has to follow the same path a perceiver has taken. In a journey to success, everyone must follow the same discipline and perseverance.

What could be Talent:

Talent is visible in one's actions, but the truth behind a talented person is their observation and perseverance. These observations help improve further action, which gradually considers one's talent. Occasionally, individuals show extraordinary abilities from their childhood in specific fields, and their observation is far better than that of their age group, which makes them skillful or gifted. One thing common in both kinds of talent, whether innate or acquired, is their way of observing surrounding events and actions. These people see things in more detail, like how things function or how certain art was created; they can notice the difference between ordinary and extraordinary actions or skills and recall those actions way better than others. These are the building blocks for any individual to develop their talent; any activity can be a talent if we put deliberate practice into it. But there is a chance that your talent may be very lucrative or just a part of your hobby.

The seed of talent lies in people's attention to specific actions or events. Every individual notices their surroundings and events differently and pays attention to particular things in different ways, and that is the seed of one's talent.

Let's take an example:

Everyone has their test of music, but some of you not only listen to the music but also notice the lyrics. Here comes someone's gift: They may not only listen to the flow of sounds but also notice how and at what intervals certain instruments are being played in the background, observing word-by-word arrangements of lyrics. This is how focus shapes talent in many cases.

Every society and Nation has deliberations of talent and rewards for that skill. For example, if you play baseball or cricket, then you have limited acceptance of your talent compared to playing soccer. Recognition of talent is dependent on geographical factors, public awareness, and information. It is very exceptional that entirely new talent comes into existence without prior information or skill sets. But in this world of technology and the internet, people are coming up with unique talents that have never been regarded as contemporary. With the help of social media and YouTube channels, new creators and audience enjoy their unique talents as well.

An example of a new genre of talent is Beatboxing creators' intricate rhythms and beats using only one's mouth and vocal cords.

Your talent is nothing more than how you look, do, and record external inputs for that specific skill set, which is always pleasant. Your focus plays a huge role in the growth of your talent.

The more aware and attentive you are to your actions, thoughts, and outside stimuli, the more they make sense in your life.

So, there are no boundaries that can define a talent area. If you constantly practice something new, one day, that will become your unique talent, and the world will know about you and your talent.

MANIFEST TALENT IN YOUR WAY

Manifestation begins with a dream, and a dream must be defined well. The strength of your dream is fueled by your longing and your emotion to see that dream come into reality.

Start your dream with the highest emotion you have

1. As you are now aware, specific talent starts with your focus area, and you are the one who can differentiate

things happening in the world. Every one of them has a different area of interest, so it is not necessary to see what you see in detail; others will see the same.

So, if your emotions are longing for something to do, do not seek the approval of others; you have a long way to go on your path of talent.

2. Clarity of your mind about your dream, the actual need to have that thing.

You may have yet to find your interest area, or you may have many fields where you are good at.

There is a need for clarity in both cases. Once you start trying different things in your life, you will find the most suitable and valuable thing to do. Your life has that choice to show the talent in the world; you are the one who decides what you want. Is it name, fame, money, or just self-actualization? Accordingly, plan your path so that, at this point, I will clear this milestone in the journey of talent development. Remember that your focus is your life energy, as are your emotions. You must correctly place this energy so that you don't get distracted.

3. Believe you deserve what you are manifesting

Sometimes, we disbelieve our capabilities or lose trust in the process of growth. All things take time, so be patient and appreciate your path.

Never think of the fruit of the tree; instead, work on soil, water, and manure. Initially, when you are imagining something big in your life, you have self-doubt. Will I succeed, or will I fail? This thought may come into your mind, but keep aside everything and believe in your decision. All decisions in our lives are neither correct nor incorrect; it is on us to make a strong decision, start working on it, and make that decision the right decision.

4. Imagine how you will cheer that achievement when you get that thing.

Until you have the fire within yourself to live the life you want, your imagination will not take full shape and size. Your longing to be successful will get some extra fuel when you imagine your upcoming life because just imagining with clear intensity releases dopamine hormones from your brain, which make you feel good and activate you to do that task with full energy.

5. Each day, add something to yourself as a prerequisite.

It is not only that your imagination and longing will make things happen; each day, you have to do something or at least take an introspection that you are on the trajectory you have planned for. Once you complete your daily practice, your brain will release another happy hormone, serotonin, and once your body gets infused with these happy hormones, no one will stop you from doing what you like doing. Day by day, your self-motivation will become part of your life, and you won't need any extra motivation from outside to do your planned things.

6. Having a sense of detachment from the result you want

Sometimes, our longing for something becomes so strong that it becomes everything in life. This obsession ultimately leads to burnout or even frustration because the results may differ from expectations. To avoid these negative outcomes, we must remember that our work is in our hands. Things may happen as we expect, or we may fail.

Life always finds its meaning if we keep on moving and doing what needs to be done, whatever is in front of us. So, you may fail and try again or try different things in life. Never be dismayed or disheartened by the things that you haven't got; if something happens, what you want is good, and if it's gone wrong, that is way better than expectation; for this to understand, you need a different perspective; and some year of the gap to know what life exactly planning for you.

Success isn't just about talent or luck or a daydream; it starts in the mind. Many of the world's most successful people didn't just work hard; they believed in their vision and the power of manifestation, and it became the reality of their lives.

Oprah Winfrey (Famous TV Host)

Oprah didn't just dream of success; she saw it long before it happened. She manifests the life she wants to live without considering her life adversities.

Oprah Winfrey's story is a masterclass in resilience and self-belief. Born in 1954 in Mississippi, she rose from poverty to become one of the most influential women in the world. *The Oprah Winfrey Show* (1986–2011) wasn't just TV—it was a movement, touching lives with deep, meaningful conversations.

She built OWN (Oprah Winfrey Network), became a powerhouse in media, and turned her success into impact, giving millions to education and social causes. Oprah proves that talent, when nurtured with grit and purpose, can change the world. Her journey is a reminder that the starting line does not matter if you have a dream to fly.

Jim Carrey's (Hollywood Actor)

Jim Carrey's journey is the perfect example of how belief fuels success. Before fame, he wrote himself a $10 million check for "acting services rendered" and carried it in his wallet. Every day, he visualized making it big—long before Hollywood knew his name.

He wasn't just dreaming; he was preparing. In 1994, that vision became reality when he landed *Dumb and Dumber*—paying exactly $10 million. Coincidence? Or is it proof that mindset shapes destiny?

Carrey's road wasn't easy. He grew up in a struggling family, even living in a van at one point. But talent, mixed with relentless belief, made him unstoppable. He broke into comedy, stole the show on *In Living Color*, and then dominated Hollywood with *Ace Ventura*, *The Mask*, and *Liar Liar*.

Arnold Schwarzenegger (Actor & Politician)

Arnold Schwarzenegger is the ultimate proof that manifestation shapes reality. Long before he became a champion bodybuilder, a Hollywood icon, or a political leader, he saw it all in his mind first.

Growing up in Austria, Arnold dreamed of moving to America and becoming the best in whatever he pursued. Through relentless training, he dominated bodybuilding, winning seven Mr. Olympia titles.

Then, he set his sights on Hollywood—despite his accent and critics doubting him. *Terminator*, *Predator*, *Total Recall*—he made it happen. Then, in true Arnold fashion, he shifted gears again, becoming the Governor of California. His story is simple but powerful.

Shah Rukh Khan (Bollywood Superstar, India)

Born into a middle-class family, **Shah Rukh Khan** came to Mumbai with a simple dream of becoming a star.

But he didn't just wish for it; he visualized it, believed it, and worked tirelessly for it. He once said, *"If you want something with all your heart, the universe conspires to help you achieve it."*

From a struggling actor to Bollywood's "King Khan," his journey is living proof that if we manifest our life and work with full spirit, nothing is unconquerable.

The lesson? Don't just wish for success; see it, believe it, and live it. Manifestation isn't magic; it's a combination of mindset, persistence, and action. What you think about, you bring it into reality.

Key Takeaways

- **Manifestation starts with a well-defined dream.** The strength of your vision depends on the emotions and passion you invest in it.

- **Your dream is unique to you.** Not everyone will see or understand your vision—trust your instincts and follow your path without seeking external validation.

- **Clarity is crucial.** Whether you have multiple interests or are still searching for your passion, exploring different paths will lead you to the right one. Define what success means to you, whether it's fame, wealth, or personal fulfillment—and plan accordingly.

- **Daily progress builds momentum.** Small, consistent actions reinforce motivation by triggering serotonin, making self-discipline and perseverance easier over time.

- **Detach from the outcome.** Obsession with results can lead to frustration. Focus on the effort, knowing that every setback is a redirection rather than a failure.

- **Mindset shapes reality.** What you think about consistently, you bring into existence. Dream, believe, take action, and success will follow.

CHAPTER 2

WHY TALENT CULTIVATION IS SIGNIFICANT

Today, most people are stuck in a rat race and do not do what they like, thoroughly enjoy their work, or feel fulfilled. They may earn money, but fulfillment is hard to earn; our actions and tasks only bring joy and fulfillment when our inner lives find expression in work.

The beauty of work is not having money or fame. Instead, we feel fulfilled when both ends meet. When our work is not to finish the task but to enjoy the overall process, and we have the satisfaction of delivering something better than our expectations, then we feel that whatever we are doing feels great, and this gives value to life.

While achieving this goal of satisfaction and life expression, our talent receives the required environment, support, and expertise in different life situations. This is an ongoing process of learning and implementing new things.

1. Self-Enrichment:

A life without purpose and inner fulfillment leads to boredom and makes us inefficient. Going through life without a goal and no sense of inner joy makes our work a burden and ultimately leads to burnout. When we give felicitation to our talent and keep on polishing it with persistence, this gives fulfillment and satisfaction. Engaging in activities that align with one's natural abilities can make us joyful and rewarded.

2. Efficiency Optimization:

Focusing on areas of talent allows individuals to excel more efficiently. When people leverage their natural strengths, tasks are often easily and effectively completed.

Only a few people excel in life, and the rest do something that they don't want to do or do it half-heartedly.

If we start doing things that we like to do or can find work that we like or something we are good at, life becomes a vacation. But what makes it difficult for most of us is that we are not able to figure out what we are capable of doing. Your talent gives you that answer.

3. Passion and Motivation:

Talents are often tied to personal passions. Pursuing activities aligned with one's talents can increase motivation and enthusiasm, driving sustained effort and dedication.

Persuading our talent gives us a natural motivation to keep on doing what we like, whatever life situation may be. We are passionate about our work and ready to face any setbacks. Because of this attitude, we become more resilient to life situations and able to go through any life situation.

4. Confidence Building:

Developing and using one's talents can boost self-confidence. Success in areas of natural ability contributes to a positive self-image and a belief in one's capabilities.

Perseverance toward talent strengthens our personality, and when we become the best at what we do, then talent gives confidence not only in what we do from our talent perspective but in the overall area of life; everything keeps on excelling in how we interact with individuals in society, how effortlessly we arrange our daily schedule and arrange our relationship with society.

Because of that self-confidence, our selection for life and life accessories changed dramatically.

5. Career Alignment:

Sometimes, we want to be what others are good at, or sometimes, we leave our strong side, observing it may not be relevant enough or won't yield money and fame, and we choose our average strength to work on, which makes money.

But the reality is different from prejudice; leaving our true side of strength makes us mediocre in life, whereas taking strong actions for identified talent and working regardless of others' opinions and throwing everything for what we do does not make you only successful, nonetheless defines Talent itself.

6. Learning and Growth

Whether you identified your talent or this comes subconsciously into your action, or talents may come naturally, ongoing development is essential. Engaging in activities that leverage one's talents encourages a mindset of continuous learning and growth.

Your learning should never stop; if you are on the path of your latent, each day has something to give you. Your awareness must be your eyes and ears to grasp something new from each day; that is how you and your talent will grow.

7. Diversity of Skills

Recognizing and nurturing various talents can lead to a diverse skill set. This versatility can be valuable in navigating different aspects of life and adapting to changing circumstances.

As your talent gets recognized in the world, your way of life changes according to how you dress, how you communicate, and how you address your life situation. Your public speaking gets much better with time, and this is because of your talent, which is getting recognized.

8. Contribution to Society:

Individuals who develop their talents often find meaningful ways to contribute to society. Whether through artistic expression, problem-solving, or leadership, talents can be harnessed for the benefit of others.

Sometimes, individual talent is shaped by the need for social, cultural, or Environmental needs.

As people grow, they see their surroundings, and accordingly, they see certain needs to change. These can be social disparity, injustice, or recognition in a particular area for national pride. Emotion drives an individual to do something great for their country, and that emotion-driven action becomes one's talent.

9. Resilience and Coping:

Being aware of one's talents can serve as a source of resilience during challenges. The confidence derived from past successes can provide a foundation for overcoming obstacles and adversity.

There are phases of life when everyone gets knocked down by life or when life becomes non-conductive. It just feels like leaving everyone around us and going for peace or a quick escape from the situation.

No matter how much effort you put into your side, things do not get the right or desired outcome. Your talent and passion help you cope with the situation, relax your mind, and give hope to start again.

You should remember that your journey is how you have come so far despite many obstacles. This life experience gives you hope that you can continue your journey and achieve the things you desire.

Key Takeaways

- **True fulfillment comes from meaningful work.** Earning money alone doesn't bring joy; real satisfaction comes when our work aligns with our inner purpose and allows us to express ourselves.

- **Talent cultivation leads to self-enrichment.** A life without purpose feels empty, but continuously developing our talents brings joy, motivation, and a sense of achievement.

- **Talent builds confidence.** Mastery in a chosen field strengthens self-belief, impacting not just our careers but also our interactions, decision-making, and overall life perspective.

- **Aligning talent with a career leads to long-term success.** Choosing a path based on natural strengths rather than external expectations results in a more fulfilling and rewarding career.

- **Talent leads to a diverse skill set.** Developing multiple talents enhances adaptability, improving communication, leadership, and problem-solving abilities over time.

- **Cultivating talent contributes to society.** Whether through art, innovation, or leadership, talent has the power to create social impact and drive positive change.

- **Talent provides resilience in difficult times.** When life gets tough, passion and past successes serve as reminders of strength, helping us navigate adversity with determination.

CHAPTER 3

SELF-DISCOVERY JOURNEY

From the beginning of your personality, since childhood, your attention is naturally drawn to certain things. You notice, remember, and act more profoundly than others on some work, which is more hectic for another person. In most cases, the journey of talent starts from childhood, where you do what you like to do, but things are different here. You do what your mind is accumulating and focusing on information, which is rewarding to the brain.

If you haven't found your talent yet, try to remember those things you noticed since childhood or you love doing some tasks without hesitation and any **exhaustion.**

Observing your thoughts and actions is the key to finding talent within yourself. Even though things are not coming into the picture, you can try some easy and effective ways to find your talent and interest.

Uncovering hidden talents and passions: -

Uncovering one's talent is the most rewarding thing in life. It is as worthwhile as finding a gold mine. Everyone wishes that their parents and friends would clap for them and that they knew their true value in life. The closer we get to our talent, the more we feel fulfilled and joyful.

Some of us find our talent sooner, whereas there are some stories where some people find their talent later in their lives, so it is not a thing on which we act in haste. Talent is not about earning a higher degree or earning money; it is more about the fulfillment of the expression of life and the satisfaction of being more valuable to the world or people around us.

TRYING THINGS AS SOON AS POSSIBLE

Many of us live mediocre lives because we cannot find what forces us to do our best and be most content. We do things maybe because our parents expect them from us or we are reasonably good at them. Lastly, we regret that we were not able to find what we were made to do.

In this condition, the best solution is to try as many things as possible; the more you try and work on over time, the more you will be able to determine for yourself whether you are made for these things or not.

Your will to do hard work will not come out because something is in trend or you are getting the attention of others; your perseverance and dedication come to their best when something extraordinary experience hits you, and you come to know that is the thing which I am born for.

And this thing will not come as early, trying a few things in life. So don't be in a rush to choose your field. Let things go a little bit slower, as well.

Childhood Interests:

Think about what you loved doing as a kid—those little things you couldn't get enough of. Chances are, they're clues to what you're naturally good at. Maybe you were the kid building epic LEGO towers, lost in a world of blocks and imagination. That could mean you've got a knack for creating, designing, or solving problems. Or maybe you were always drawing, painting, or crafting—your creative side might be your superpower. If you were the one organizing games or leading the pack, leadership and planning could be your thing. Did you love puzzles or strategy games? Your brain is probably wired for logic and problem-solving. And if you were the kid with your nose in a book or scribbling stories, words and ideas might be your jam. Whatever it was, those childhood passions are like little breadcrumbs leading you back to what lights you up. Revisit them, lean into those skills, and see where they take you now.

Feedback:

Ask friends, family, and colleagues about activities or skills they believe you excel in. Sometimes, we are not aware of our talents, but people around us notice which tasks we do best. You can ask your friends and family members to give a quick assessment of your skilled field, and you can consider those points to find your talent. We are all well aware that people around us have always observed our actions. Take advantage of the people.

Try new activities:

One thing you can do to find your talent area is to do something new that you haven't even tried yet, such as sports, creativity, music, or group or community activities. Keep on experimenting with things and find what gives you a sense of pleasantness and is sustainable for you. Do not leave any chances to help others because, in the process of helping others, you use all your skills and even learn and help others. Each volunteer activity will introduce and add some more knowledge to you, and this may give you a clue to know your talent.

Seek Inspiration:

Look for inspiration from role models or individuals who excel in areas that interest you. As you grow up, you find some person more competent, and you want to be like them. They can be an actor or actresses, a businessman, a politician, or a hairdresser. They can be anyone who has drawn your attention, and this happens not because you think they are successful or have lots of money. Most of the time, it is your inner talent that wants to sprout out, and that one is just finding its possibilities.

Do these 5-minute activities when you feel Peaceful and full of Energy.

Objective	Task
1. Passion Mapping Identify personal passion and Interests.	Reflect and write down answers to these questions:
	What excites you the most right now?
	What were your passions as a kid, teen, or adult?
2. Inspiration Journal Explore new opportunities.	List activities or accomplishments of others that make you think, "Wish I would be like this."
3. Skill Assessment Recognize personal strengths.	What have you become good at over the years?
	What skills have you acquired?

4. Freedom Exercise Visualize a life with no restrictions.	Write about what you would do tomorrow if you had no responsibilities.
5. Help & Expertise Understand your unique value.	What do others come to you for help with?
	What do you accomplish quickly that takes others a long time?

Key Takeaways

- **Your childhood holds clues to your talent.** The things you loved doing as a child- playing, drawing, organizing, or solving puzzles can help you find your natural strengths.

- **Finding your talent takes time.** There's no need to rush. The more you explore and try different things, the easier it becomes to discover what excites you.

- **Trying new things helps.** Experiment with different activities, music, creative projects, or leadership roles to see what feels natural and enjoyable.

- **Look at who inspires you.** The people you often admire reflect something inside you. Please pay

attention to what attracts you to them. It might be a
hint about your talent.

- **Do simple exercises to understand yourself better.**
Writing down your interests, skills, and dreams can
help you see what truly matters to you.

Chapter 4

Nurturing Your Talents

Creating a supportive environment for talent development

Maybe someone is talented in his way of doing things, but contribution to each day's progress matters the most. Some fortunate individuals have all the facilities that are required to nurture their talent, and most of them have to find ways to make a conducive environment for their talent.

Arrangements give some an initial advantage, and others have excuses, but those who have the fire burning within them find their way.

If you are discouraged by not having arrangements and finding an unfriendly environment, then you are making excuses for yourself. Ultimately, your dedication and full effort matter the most in finding, nurturing, and defining talent.

Defining talent means you are the one who is not going the same way as the world has gone through; in a way, you are making new terrain for future generations to go your way.

Never go with the trend:

You may find something that others are doing, and you too can effortlessly do and enjoy other appreciation, but you may kill your talent. Often, other appreciation may take you far from your true value. You must look up to your nature, which any kind of materialism or acknowledgment should not influence.

Your talent must define you and your expression of joy and perception. Take time, be patient, and check yourself on whether you want to impress others or what you are expressing, which is pouring itself. The world has enough space for anything, and you need not adopt others' styles and skills to have a successful life.

Keeping secrets of others: This is one trait of human personality that has been least talked about, whereas this one trend is highly valuable for life. We humans emotionally depend on one another to a large extent, and this dependency can be beautiful if we keep our sharing and caring consciously.

A good listener does not just listen with an involvement but also keeps someone's secret as their treasure; this practice makes you the most reliable person in anyone's life, and this kind of honor to any person makes you the most valuable person in someone's life.

This bonding allowed someone to share their hidden truth and experience of life.

Sometimes, the most valuable life experiences and lessons are hidden in someone's heart. However, you can have that valuable thing in your life without going through the same hard situations that person has gone through. By gaining the truth of life, you don't make the same mistakes, and you save yourself from many bitter and painful life lessons. This can be your add-on feature to talent.

Cherish your failure

If you are constantly doing something and not getting your desired result, it doesn't mean you should quit; if your failure is giving you satisfaction and fueling you to take the next try, then it is an indication that you are exploring your true talent. If setbacks fire you up and make you want to try again, that's not failure—it's a sign you're on the right path.

True talent isn't about easy wins; it's about loving the process. The drive to keep going, even without quick results, shows you're onto something real. Every "miss" is practice, every frustration a lesson. Mastery is built through stubborn, joyful repetition.

Perseverance: - You may have natural talent, but it'll be surpassed by someone else's hard work if you don't have perseverance. Talent alone isn't enough—it's just the starting point. Think of it like a diamond; even the most precious stone needs to be cut, polished, and refined to reveal its true value. Without that effort, it stays rough and undervalued. The same goes for your skills.

The more you practice, refine, and push yourself, the more you'll shine. Persistence turns potential into mastery. So, don't just rely on what comes naturally. Put in the work, stay consistent, and watch how far you can go.

Do Not Take Insults Seriously

There will be moments in your life when you're learning a new skill and failing over and over again. People around you might laugh. Not because they're cruel, but because to them, it's just a passing joke. They're having fun at the moment, but you think they'll remember it forever. The truth is, they won't.

You're the only one holding on to it. Once you master that skill, those same people will admire you and celebrate your success. That's just how life works.

Your failures aren't the end; they're lessons pushing you to grow. Every mistake is just a step forward, a chance to sharpen your craft. Keep going, even when the world seems to be watching and laughing. One day, the same audience will cheer for you.

Once you reach the top of that hill, the laughter will turn into applause. Remember, failure is never final—it's just part of the process that builds the strength you need to succeed. Stay with it. You've got this.

The role of education and continuous learning.

Education gives holistic support to one's talent; this is like salt in a recipe; no matter how good the food is, if you miss putting salt into it, the test of that recipe will go in vain. Your education doesn't mean the years you spend in school and college. Still, it depends on the quality of knowledge you gathered over time and how efficiently you are applying that knowledge in everyday life situations. Our learning is not limited to school, college, or books we have read; our life is a classroom by itself, and this classroom no one can escape. Those who learn and value the lessons of life will become the fortunate ones.

ENERGY MANAGEMENT IS MORE RELEVANT THAN TIME MANAGEMENT

You may think managing time is the key, but you should change your perspective. If you learn to manage your body and its energy, you can finish a task that takes ten hours in six hours. This is only possible if your body has the right kind of fuel.

So, food management is one aspect of energy management, and a suitable daily routine is another. Physical exercise is also beneficial for mental health.

Mindfulness Practices:

You can start practicing mindfulness or Yoga to learn what you want to do. These practices have helped many people find their true talents because mindful practices close the external world and reveal the things that you have in abundance inside you. In our world, there are too many things to do, and this may confuse anyone about what the best option is. As you keep a distance from the external world, things become clearer.

Spirituality and Talent Development:

Spirituality is not a set of belief systems; this is a way of doing things consciously rather than believing in a god or any scriptures. This is simple yet contains many depths and dimensions for those who want to explore it.

The point is that we need to be spiritual. We are all spiritual, whether believers or atheists. Spirituality's core practice is aligning our human system with this large cosmic existence and its functions. Whether you agree with this or not, you cannot deny that when you align your lifestyle with sunrise and sunset, your body functions best when you wake up early in the morning and do some workout or Yoga.

You may not consider yourself spiritual, but spirituality already includes everyone. Spirituality will become part of your experience when you dive deeper into it. The more you become aware, the more you will find its presence.

For example, how many times a day are we aware that we are living on a planet moving at a very high speed or that we are just a very small piece of this planet walking here and there? This planet holds zillions of lives and nurses them. This is how spirituality has included us.

When you include some spiritual practices in your everyday life, you will never regret your decision. Health is the first thing that comes into your life, and after that, there are many more benefits and pleasant experiences that it offers to everyone.

Some of the benefits that it gives you are the chances of getting addicted to drugs and alcohol or any other substance become very minimal, and these are the things that can destroy someone's life very easily. No matter how talented you are, once you get addicted to anything like this, your life will no longer be on your command. Now, you become a slave of your addiction.

Spirituality: Your Parallel Life

At present, the whole world has two parallel lives: a virtual or digital life and a personal and professional life. We all know that everyone's virtual life seems brighter and happier than their original life.

Almost everyone shows that their life is much happier than others, but in reality, they are more exhausted. As you work day and night for your materialistic life, take one more step and create a parallel spiritual life as well.

Why is it important to have a parallel life?

Let's understand this with a simple example: suppose you are a national-level athlete and preparing for the Olympic games, but somehow you are banned by the federation for that condition. You may go into depression and keep on regrating over time as things happen to you.

When life throws unexpected things at you, spiritual practices can help you remain stable and sound. You know from your experiences that happiness does not depend upon external things; life itself is a happier phenomenon. With this stability, you can move in any direction if things are not under your control.

Nature vs. Nurture: Many people have certain skills from an early age, and despite this, they have practiced that skill more than anyone else; maybe nature gives someone an advantage, but nurturing that talent is the sole responsibility of an individual.

Take the example of **Usain Bolt,** the fastest man in the world. Bolt displayed speed early on but underwent rigorous training to perfect his technique. Despite his natural athleticism, his coaches pushed him through intense sprint drills and strength training. His success was as much a product of practice as of his natural speed.

And we can take one more example of **Mozart** (Composer and Musician)

Mozart showed early musical talent, but his father, Leopold, a musician and teacher, implemented strict training. Mozart practiced piano and violin intensely for hours each day, developing his skills and composing ability from a young age. His dedication to music and rigorous practice were key to his genius.

This example shows us that even if we have certain talents within us, it takes a lot of practice to become world-class.

Comfort Zone Overwrite: The human brain is designed so that a new process or environment is likely to overwhelm most people, and they think they cannot endure it. However, when time is spent on the same thing, the brain becomes accommodated, and people start enjoying things that they were too afraid to do and feeling incompetent.

Initially, if you are feeling overwhelmed or things are going over your head, don't worry. It is a normal human sign. Take your task or skill day by day; just be patient and regular to take it to the finish line, and the thing that seems too big to you becomes part of yourself.

If you try to be in the same circle of your comfort zone, then it will shrink one day, and you will find that your ability is not what it used to be, and gradually, you will shift to shorter areas of the game and so on. On the other hand, you will get some strength to face the problem head-on, and you will succeed in your task.

Your brain will release adrenaline hormones, and this boozy, bumpy feeling is amazing. So, resting and taking time is another thing, but when it comes to facing the problem that needs to be addressed, do it in your style and have your reward by the brain.

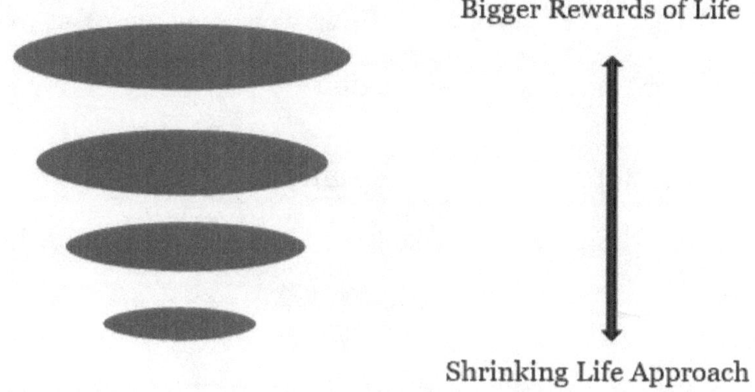

Key Takeaways

- **Create Your Growth Environment** – Don't wait for ideal conditions; build your own space to nurture your talent.

- **Define Your Path** – Avoid chasing trends; express your talent in a way that feels authentic to you.

- **Ignore Insults and Stay Focused** – People may laugh at your failures, but once you succeed, they'll admire you.

- **Education Goes Beyond School** – True learning is about applying knowledge to real-life situations.

- **Energy Management Over Time Management** – Your efficiency depends on how well you manage your energy, not just your schedule.

- **Spirituality Enhances Resilience** – Being spiritually aware helps you stay stable and focused through life's ups and downs.

- **Step Outside Your Comfort Zone** – Growth happens when you challenge yourself; what feels overwhelming today will become second nature with time.

Chapter 5

Goal Setting And Planning

All of us fall and fail many times in the process of learning. That's part of the journey. However, the key difference between those who grow and those who give up lies in one thing: your mindset, longing to stay on the process, and your confined roadmap of success. It's not just about having a dream; it's about turning that dream into a reality.

Planning is a talent in itself, and the truth is we all have it to some degree. From small tasks in our daily routine, like planning what to eat or what time to wake up, to long-term goals like where we want to be in five or ten years, big multinational companies plan for their break-even that may go for 20 years and more.

But the real magic happens when you align your personal goals with your identified talents. This is where life truly starts to change.

<u>**The Two Pillars of Goal Setting**</u>

When it comes to setting meaningful goals, they need to meet two basic requirements to stand the test of time: **life fulfillment** and **material well-being**.

1. **Life Fulfilment:** This is the part that makes your soul happy. It's about doing something that feels right at your core, something that excites you, challenges you, and makes you want to jump out of bed in the morning. Life fulfillment means your talent isn't just a means to an end; it's a source of joy, curiosity, and growth. Without this, life feels empty, and all the things around us are burdens and liabilities to manage. Our lives do not shine if we take our liabilities too seriously. But when we feel joyful while serving others, it makes sense of fulfillment.

2. **Material Well-being:** Let's be honest! Passion alone isn't enough to sustain you in life. Your goals should also support your materialistic needs. This doesn't mean you need to be a billionaire, but your talent should give you stability and security, and all the basic

things should be taken care of. Whether it's providing a steady income or opening doors to new opportunities, make sure your plans include your material well-being and that you can meet the needs of your family as well.

When your talent and goals check both areas of life, that's when you find true balance.

Process of Goal Setting

It's easy to talk about setting goals, but how do you do it? Here's a simple, step-by-step process to help you turn your talent into a plan:

1. Identify Your Talent: You've already done the hard part, discovering what you're good at. Now, it's time to get clear on how far you want to take it. Ask yourself: *What do I want to achieve with this talent? How can it improve my life and the lives of others? Whatever I am doing right now, at the end of my life, will all this make sense at that time?*

2. Set Clear Goals: Be specific; instead of saying, *I want to be successful,* define what success looks like to you. Is it starting your own business? Becoming a top performer in any technical field? Beating the previous record of any Athlete? Teaching others what you've learned? Make your goals as detailed as possible.

3. Break It Into Small Steps: Big goals can feel overwhelming, so breaking them down into smaller, manageable steps and doing everything at once may confuse you. Focus on what you can do today, this week, and this month. Each step forward builds momentum, which keeps you going even when things get tough. Doing things in small steps always brings bigger and better results.

4. Stay Flexible: Life rarely goes according to plan. Goals evolve, situations change, and setbacks are guaranteed. That's okay. Be ready to adjust your plan without losing sight of your specific dream. Flexibility is not a failure—it's wisdom. Never get agitated or angry in life situations. This will reduce your adaptability to change.

The more you become flexible, the stronger your personality will shape itself.

5. Track Your Progress: Introspection for your growth is very crucial to strength talent. Are you getting closer to your goal? Note down your learning between the process, Celebrate the small wins, and learn from the results. Small progress also counts; no matter how slow you are moving, that still counts progress.

The Power of Patience and Persistence

Goal setting and planning are not one-time activities. They're ongoing processes that require patience, persistence, and plenty of self-reflection. Don't make a benchmark of others; first, evaluate your environment and your standing ground. It's easy to get discouraged by looking at other's progress, but you should also think that everyone does have the same starting line. When things don't happen as quickly as you'd like, just be patient and keep on going.

Every stumble, every mistake, and every delay is part of your journey. Keep refining your goals as you learn more about yourself and your talent. The path may not be a straight line, but as long as you stay committed, you'll get where you're meant to be.

Goal setting and planning aren't just about reaching a destination. It's also about enjoying the progress of learning. They're about becoming the kind of person who knows how to dream big, take bold steps, and turn setbacks into stepping stones. Once you reach that hilltop, all the hard work will be worth it. When you look back on your journey, you will know that each sacrifice you have made in the process is worth doing.

Key Takeaways

- **Planning is a Talent** – Everyone can plan, whether for small tasks or long-term goals.

- **Align Goals with Talent** – True success happens when personal goals align with your natural abilities.

- **Be Specific About Success** – Clearly define what success looks like for you instead of unclear aspirations.

- **Break Big Goals into Steps** – Small, consistent actions lead to massive progress over time.

- **Flexibility is Key** – Plans may change, and adaptability is a strength, not a failure.

- **Track Your Progress** – Celebrate small wins, learn from setbacks, and adjust as needed.

- **Patience and Persistence Matter** – Success is an ongoing process requiring self-reflection and perseverance.

Chapter 6

Building a Personal Brand

Leveraging talents for personal branding.

Whatever is more visible and attractive to the world is branding. The more you become presentable to the world, the more your brand value increases.

Even if you are very skilled but you are not visible or presentable in the present world, you can never make yourself a brand that shines in the sky. Your branding is as important as your talent; if you are unable to make your talent presentable, you may not earn a living well. But if you can make your talent a brand, then you will not get earnings but much more than your expectation.

Love and recognition from all over the world will be a blessing that will be poured on you; you will become part of the global family that you never expected and experienced. Branding is not just selling your talent to this world; branding is something that reflects you and your inner values.

Authenticity: A Core Value

Your authenticity is the heart of your brand. Never add or subtract anything that doesn't feel true to your core. The world will try to mold you, but staying genuine sets you apart. Don't chase trends or force something that doesn't align with you. Real connection comes from being real. Trust that your unique essence is enough—it's what will attract the right people and opportunities. Stay honest, stay true, and your authenticity will be your greatest strength.

While building your talent, always focus on what makes you unique. Whatever skill you pursue, you'll face competition. The key is finding the sweet spot between what you love and what your audience values. If you miss that connection, your growth will feel meaningless, and you'll struggle to stay motivated. It may take a little more time to look into your talent and how you can expand it to all possible opportunities that the world is offering right now.

Your Audience Matter

Remember, people who support and admire your talent are the ones who turn your hard work into recognition, opportunities, and rewards. Every talent needs to thrive. Communicate your unique value and show the world what sets you apart, and success will follow naturally. Stay true to yourself, but never lose sight of the bigger picture—your audience matters.

In marketing, there's a term called **USP—Unique Selling Proposition**. It's about what makes a product or brand stand out, and the same principle applies to your talent. Your **uniqueness is your identified talent**, your brand. It's what sets you apart from the crowd. Focus on what makes you different and how that difference connects with what people want or need.

Identify the gap by assessing your skills—what you have, what you lack, and how you compare to others. Seek feedback from mentors, friends, or family, then work on those inputs and set clear goals.

Highlight your uniqueness by showcasing your strengths and understanding what your audience truly needs. Sometimes, a small adjustment can elevate your impact. Talent development is a two-way process—growing your skills while creating value for others. Stay dynamic, keep learning, and deliver fresh results consistently. When people feel they're gaining value from your work, your talent will naturally grow and thrive.

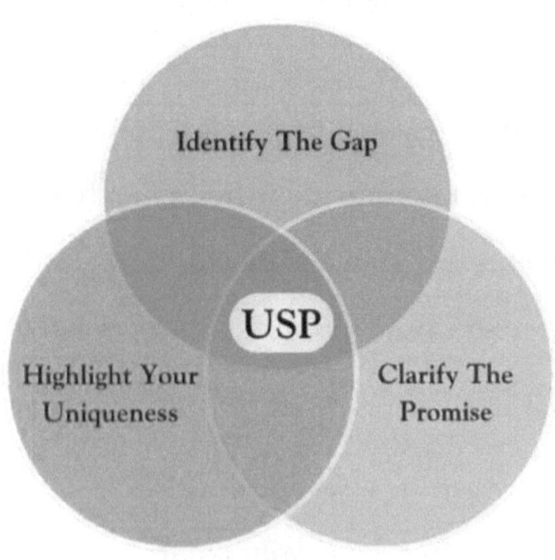

1.   Identifying the Gap: Make a self-assessment of what you have and what you lack in your respective field. Evaluate your skills in comparison to others, your weaknesses, and where you fit in.

Try to get feedback from your friends, family members, coach, or mentor. Once you get your input, work on them and set a benchmark.

2.   Highlight Your Uniqueness: Present whatever you have learned in your journey in the best way possible. Sometimes, you work hard on your skills, but you won't get much out of them. You must understand the audience and what they want. Your little bit of correction will take you to the next level.

3.   Clarify The Promise: - This is a two-way process. One is the growth of your talent, and the other one is impacting, benefiting, and touching other's lives in a way that they are getting what they were expecting fulfillment in their life. Talent development is a dynamic process where you may change and adopt new skills and methods. You have to learn in day-to-day life and keep on practicing and

delivering something new all the time. This makes your target audience where they feel they are getting value from your results.

Key Takeaways

- **Branding = Visibility + Value** – No matter how talented you are, if you're not visible, your skills won't make an impact. Your talent must be presented in a way that captures attention and creates value.

- **Authenticity is Everything** – Stay true to yourself. Don't follow trends that don't align with your values. Real connection and long-term success come from being genuine.

- **Your Audience is Your Strength** – The people who support and recognize your talent are the ones who help you grow. Engage with them, understand their needs, and deliver value consistently.

- **Identify the Gap** – Self-assess your skills, strengths, and areas for improvement. Get feedback and use it to refine your approach.

- **Showcase What Makes You Stand Out** – Hard work alone isn't enough. Present your skills in a way that speaks directly to what your audience is looking for.

- **Talent Development is a Two-Way Street** – Your growth should also create value for others. Keep learning, evolving, and delivering something fresh to stay relevant and impactful.

Chapter 7

Overcoming Challenges

hallenges never come in our life to destroy us but come to discover our potential."

Life without a problem is gloomy.

Suppose you are playing a game and you have no hurdle, no next hard level to cross and think upon. You are not crossing any difficulty, nor do you have any next level to cross. Will you continue to play that game?

The answer is no!

Why? Because you are not using your skill, creative thinking, or developing out-of-the-box ideas.

This is the same with life. If we continue doing something without difficulty for a long time, we will need to refresh ourselves; otherwise, it will become monotonous and boring.

We should always remember that life has problems, not suffering. We all have some problems, and this is inevitable, but we all have a choice about whether to handle them consciously or make them an ongoing suffering. Sometimes, our minds do not work for us but against us.

We start overthinking the problem and keep thinking about it, and this very unpleasant thought becomes a painful emotion. We carry this emotion for a long time, and this long period of suffering is as long as we think.

The more we think, the bigger and bigger it becomes. So, thinking is a choice, and problems are just situations. Your competency will determine the level of solution you get.

The more you get stressed about it, the more substandard the quality of the solution will be. On the other hand, if you can manage yourself well in harsh circumstances, you will easily come out of the problem and feel like a champion.

There are many obstacles to talent acquisition. If a talented person is not watchful of these obstacles, they may lose their talent or opportunity to thrive.

- Lack of discipline and irregular routine: - No matter how talented someone is, if they are not disciplined, they may become an obstacle, and their intelligence turns against them. The more energy they have, the more struggle they may face.

- Perfectionism: Our instinct for perfectionism is there because we are more of ourselves in our imagination. However, things become problematic when we do not embrace our continuous improvement and do not realize that imagination is a quicker thing than crafting imagination into reality. Going step by step and having fractional goals for the intended result is the best way to go.

Being imperfect is not a matter of shame; every work has some flaw, and we should appreciate our growth. Chasing unrealistic perfection demotivates and causes procrastination.

- Not managing negative critics: The most effective way to manage negative critics is to pass the word as it is. Many people in the world love trolling others, sometimes for their cheap happiness and sometimes to demotivate you. This is on us and how we are responding to them. If we show that we are affected by them, they will get encouragement for what they do. So, the best way to tackle this problem is not to get distracted at all.

The second way to do that is to calm down and assess whether you need to work on something or focus on what you are doing.

Never waste your time in justifying everyone and seeking approvals.

- Neglecting Gut Health: Our lives are the result of the food we ingest over time. How energetic or lethargic we are mostly depends on two things: how we manage our negative emotions and our food habits. Let's examine our gut and its health.

Gut Microbiome: Most people think the human body is made up of human cells only, but the truth is quite different. A study published in PLOS Biology in 2016 revised the number of bacterial cells in the body. The researchers estimated that the body contains approximately 30 trillion human cells and about 38 trillion bacterial cells, a nearly 1:1 ratio.

Even with this huge number, the total mass of bacterial cells is nearly 0.2 kg because they are much smaller than human cells. Seventy percent of them inhabit our colon region. Some of them are good for our system, and some of them cause diseases.

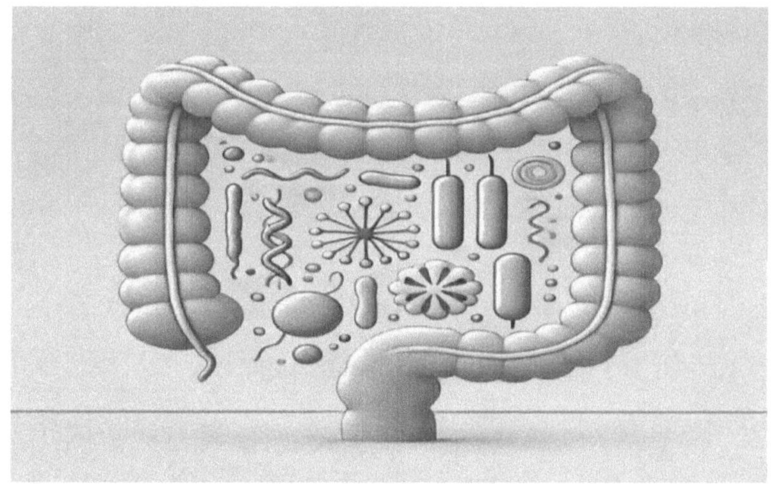

New research on the Gut Microbiome and its effect on the mind is uncovering new findings every day. Good food is not what tests good; instead, good food makes the body feel great. Digestion and after-digestion are equally important. Take care of your test as well as your gut; this will reward your body and mind. Nowadays, the gut is considered our second brain because the better the gut condition, the better the mind responds.

A simple way to check our Gut Biome is to observe how pleasant your mood is and how light your body is; this lightness means less friction while doing any activity.

If you take care of your gut biome, this will help you deal with your procrastination and dullness. If your gut is not healthy enough, you may feel hazy in your body, and your mind may feel congested in the thought process.

The more you become careful about it and observe yourself, the more naturally you will shift to the ideal diet and food choices. One must be concerned that a healthy Gut is a fundamental ground for your talent to thrive. No matter which kind of opportunity you are exposed to, if you are not able to manage your Healthy Gut, in the long run, things will go wrong, and you will become a lazy, anxious, and depressed person.

It is truly hard to count external challenges. There can be as many as you can think of, but better vision and readiness help us respond to them. If we work on ourselves, then managing unprecedented things becomes easier.

Key Takeaways

- **Challenges Reveal Potential** – Problems aren't meant to break you but to unlock your hidden strengths. Just like a game without levels is boring, life without challenges lacks growth.

- **Suffering is a Choice**. Problems are inevitable, but how you handle them is in your control. Overthinking turns problems into prolonged suffering, so manage your thoughts wisely.

- **Quality of Thought = Quality of Solution**. Stress weakens one's ability to solve problems. Stay composed, and one will find better, more effective solutions.

- **Your Gut is Your Second Brain** – A well-balanced gut microbiome improves mood, creativity, and productivity. Poor gut health can lead to lethargy, anxiety, and a foggy mind.

- **Mastering Internal Challenges Strengthens External Readiness** – The better you manage yourself, the easier it is to handle unexpected difficulties.

CHAPTER 8

BALANCING PASSION AND PRACTICALITY

If you have a clear mindset, then every challenge will add some fruitful results to your journey of growth. If you are confused or letting things be a burden, you will end up with all opportunities with a problem and a failure.

Lack of clarity on specifying talent- It may be possible that you are good in many activities and have more skill sets than others. Still, you must choose one that does not lose your interest in the long run and becomes irrelevant in the future.

Everyone should work on their clarity before making the final decision about what they will pursue in life.

Steve, job on clarity

- Focus and simplicity: "That's been one of my mantras-focus and simplicity. Simple can be harder than complex: You have to work hard to get your thinking clean to make it simple. But it's worth it in the end because once you get there, you can move mountains".

Our life has situations, not problems; it is on us how we see different situations as problems or a chance to prove ourselves.

Let us see how Elon Musk and his ventures successfully navigated this balance.

From a very young age, Elon made books as his best companion; at the age of ten, he taught computer programming, and at the age of 12, he sold his first computer game. His early life had some struggles, too, but he continued with full determination. One of the best habits that everyone should be reading and implementing. He created today's super successful space venture out of his ambition for innovation; his first world-renowned success was PayPal, which revolutionized the online payment system.

His progressive life led him to create Tesla, SpaceX, and The Boring Company, which is developing

Hyperloop and underground road tunnels. He then bought Twitter/X.

Engineering Passion and Vision

Elon Musk's passion for engineering is distinct from identifying the Gap and providing solutions to the problem. Unlike other businessmen, he dreams of something challenging and breaking the current barrier of trend. He hardly relies on current industrial knowledge, which is why he dares to think and bring about innovation in engineering and management of the enterprise.

Tesla: - Revolutionizing Electric Vehicles

Before Tesla, no one dreamed that EVs could become a desirable symbol of luxury and a state-of-the-art sports car. Later on, the company provided many car segments for the general public, too; now, Tesla is making different commercial EVs that are sustainable modes of transport.

Tesla has innovated battery technology and autonomous driving in their cars. Musk insisted engineers build a car that could drive autonomously with the help of AI and outperform gasoline vehicles in both range and speed.

Tesla has also expanded beyond cars, developing energy solutions like powerwall home batteries and solar energy products. The company's Gigafactories produce batteries and vehicles at scale, helping reduce costs and accelerate EV adoption globally.

SpaceX: - Lowering the Cost of Space Travel

When Elon Musk talked about reusable rockets, no one believed that this was possible. However, he used all his Engineering Knowledge and intensively studied rocket science, then formed a team that believed in his dream. In 2008, SpaceX became the first private company to send a liquid-fueled rocket (Falcon 1) into orbit. This journey continued, and Falcon 9 and Falcon Heavy were used for deep space exploration. One space program is specially dedicated to the colonization of Planet Mars through Starship.

Starlink is a dedicated project that uses small satellites to cover the entire Earth. These satellites enable remote parts of the world to access high-speed internet.

Bridging Innovation and Business Success

Elon Musk's companies not only invent and innovate but also well commercialize their product and services. He made and broke several industrial morns, such as cost-cutting and reusable rockets in SpaceX. His ability to combine engineering expertise with business implementation is very rare, and that is what defines his success.

Key Takeaways

- **Clarity is Key** – If you have a clear vision, challenges become stepping stones. Without clarity, even opportunities can feel like burdens.

- **Focus and Simplicity** – Inspired by Steve Jobs' mantra, clarity in thinking leads to impactful actions and innovation.

- **Situations vs. Problems** – Life presents situations; it's up to you to see them as obstacles or opportunities for growth.

- **Innovation + Business Mindset** – Success isn't just about passion; it's about identifying gaps, providing solutions, and scaling them effectively.

- **Think Beyond Trends**: Musk's ventures, such as Tesla, SpaceX, and Starlink, succeeded because he focused on breaking barriers rather than following industry norms.

- **Implementation is Everything** – Vision without execution is meaningless; turning ideas into reality is what defines true success.

Chapter 9

Embracing Continuous Growth

Relevance in a fast-moving world isn't about knowing everything; it's about staying open to growth. The most successful people aren't the ones who resist change but those who see it as an invitation to evolve.

1. **The Power of Introspection**

- Challenges push us to look inward, analyze our actions, and reflect on past decisions.

- This self-examination reconnects us with a higher consciousness that has always been present.

- Growth happens not because of deliberate procedures but because of an ongoing connection with self-awareness.

2. Spirituality and Consciousness

- Spirituality is not about rigid beliefs or religious rituals; it is about being fully present.

- Whether you believe in a higher power or not, self-awareness and mindfulness make you a spiritual being.

- Being conscious of our actions and thoughts helps us grow continuously.

3. Neuroplasticity: The Brain's Lifelong Ability to Adapt

Our brain never truly gets old—it continues to learn, adapt to new environments, and acquire new skills throughout life. **Neuroplasticity** refers to the brain's ability to reorganize itself by forming and strengthening neural connections in response to new experiences and learning. Through continuous practice, neuroplasticity allows the brain to become more efficient by reinforcing important neural pathways and eliminating unnecessary ones.

This ability is most effective during childhood and adolescence, but it remains active throughout life. Regular mental exercises, a healthy diet, and continuous learning can support neuroplasticity and keep the brain functioning at its best. According to current research, our brain has roughly **100 trillion synapses** and about **86 billion neurons**, all working together to process and store information.

4. The Role of Synapses in Learning and Growth

Synapses are crucial for everything the brain does—from thinking and learning to feeling emotions and controlling the body. They act like tiny switches that turn signals on or off, shaping how information flows through the brain.

With learning and practice, synapses can grow stronger or form new connections, improving skills and memory. Conversely, unused synapses weaken and disappear over time in a process called **synaptic pruning**. This adaptability is a key part of how the brain grows, changes, and stays efficient throughout life.

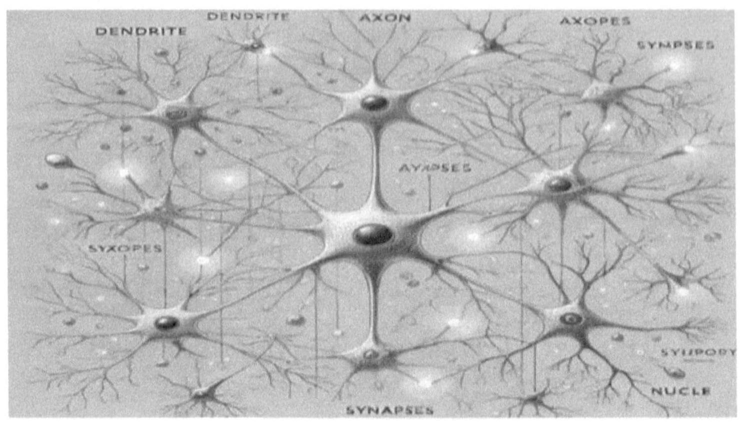

5. Functional Plasticity: The Brain's Ability to Adapt After Damage

Our brains have special abilities, one of the most essential of which is **functional plasticity**—the ability to transfer the work of a damaged part of the brain to a healthier region. This remarkable feature ensures that the brain can reorganize and continue functioning even after injury.

Key Aspects of Functional Plasticity:

- **Compensation After Damage:** If a specific brain region is injured (e.g., due to a stroke), other parts of the brain can take over lost functions, such as movement, speech, or memory.

- **Reorganization:** Neurons and brain circuits adapt to perform roles they weren't initially designed for. For example, in blind individuals, the visual cortex may process touch or sound stimuli, enhancing their ability to navigate the world through other senses.

6. **Adapting to Change**

- The world is constantly evolving, and staying rigid leads to stagnation.

- Our brains are built to adapt—this is called neuroplasticity. Every time we learn something new or push ourselves outside our comfort zone, our neural pathways reorganize, making us more resilient and capable.

- Functional plasticity proves that even when faced with challenges—whether physical, mental, or emotional—our brains can find new ways to function. If our brains can adapt at such a deep level, imagine what we can achieve by embracing change rather than confronting it.

- Growth is about learning from setbacks rather than avoiding them. The more we challenge ourselves, the stronger our minds become.

7. Self-Compassion in Growth

- Mistakes are not failures; they are lessons in disguise.

- Growth requires patience and self-kindness during struggles.

- The biggest transformations happen when we see obstacles as stepping stones.

8. Growth as a Journey, Not a Destination

- There is no final point in personal growth; it is a continuous process.

- Every experience—good or bad—contributes to our transformation.

- By embracing curiosity, resilience, and self-awareness, we turn every moment into an opportunity for growth.

By approaching life with an open mind and a willingness to adapt, we not only grow but thrive.

Continuous growth is about becoming a better version of ourselves every day.

Key Takeaways

- Growth comes from taking responsibility for both successes and failures.

- Self-awareness and introspection are powerful tools for continuous improvement.

- Neuroplasticity allows the brain to learn, adapt, and form new neural connections throughout life.

- Synaptic pruning helps the brain stay efficient by strengthening useful connections and eliminating unused ones.

- Functional plasticity enables the brain to recover from injuries by redistributing tasks to healthier areas.

- Adapting to change and cultivating a lifelong learning mindset enhances personal and cognitive growth.

CHAPTER 10

GIVING BACK AND IMPACTING OTHERS

The role of talent in making a positive impact on others

Our journey is the best we can go, and if it is considered that it will give value to the world and be appreciated, it leaves a trail and a story for many to inspire and follow their passion. A success story has a legacy, and a successor carries that legacy. At the end of a story, a new story is born, and we humans not only enjoy what we have; we also enjoy it when we share what we have.

One of the greatest rewards in someone's life is to serve others through their work and talent. The more we grow, the more we want to deliver any form of knowledge, wealth, or service.

Role of a mentor

Shaping raw talent into a shining star takes time, patience, and guidance. There's a famous saying: *"Time is the greatest teacher, and no one can buy it."* This couldn't be truer when it comes to mastering a skill.

A mentor plays a key role in talent growth. Their experience, wisdom, and hard-earned knowledge—gained through years of dedication—make them powerful guides.

They help you navigate challenges and accelerate your progress. A good mentor becomes an invaluable asset in your journey.

However, even if you don't have a mentor, life will eventually shape you into one. If you're committed to a skill long enough, time will become your teacher. Every stumble, every small victory, and every lesson learned will make you wiser.

One day, you'll look back and realize you've gained the same depth of knowledge that only time and experience can provide. The key is to stay consistent and open to learning. Whether through a mentor or life itself, growth is inevitable if you keep going.

Mentorship and sharing knowledge with the community.

Whatever we learn in our long journey to being talented in any field of life, we want to give it back to the world in a more systematic way and achievable way.

Our experience and expertise that we have gained through our hard work, analysis, and findings is what works and what doesn't work. It saves the time and effort of others; a great mentor is a great learner, and a great learner becomes a great mentor.

Building a Legacy Through Talent

Talent is more than just personal success—it's about the difference we make in the lives of others. A true legacy is built when we use our skills, knowledge, and experiences to inspire, guide, and uplift those around us. Every step we take to grow creates a path for someone else to follow. Success isn't just about reaching the top; it's about helping others climb as well.

As we develop our talents, we naturally feel the need to share what we've learned. Whether it's through teaching, mentoring, or leading by example, our knowledge becomes more valuable when it helps others grow.

The best creators, leaders, and innovators don't just achieve—they pass on what they've learned, making the journey easier for the next generation.

No one builds a legacy alone. Those who came before us shaped the world we live in, and now it's our turn to do the same for those who come after us. The more we give—whether it's wisdom, experience, or support—the more lasting our impact becomes.

A true legacy isn't about fame or recognition. It's about using our talents to create something meaningful that continues to grow, inspire, and serve others long after we're gone.

Key Takeaways

- Talent **becomes meaningful when shared.** True success is not just about personal achievement but about creating value for others and inspiring future generations.

- **Mentorship accelerates growth.** A mentor's experience and wisdom help shape raw talent into greatness. Even without a mentor, life itself will guide those who remain committed to learning.

- **Great learners become great mentors.** The knowledge and expertise we gain through years of practice should be passed on to others in a structured and accessible way, making their journey smoother.

- **Building a legacy goes beyond personal success.** The real impact of talent is measured by how it helps others grow, innovate, and overcome challenges.

- **No one builds a legacy alone.** Every success story is built on the lessons and contributions of those who came before. By sharing what we know, we create a ripple effect of growth and inspiration.

- **Giving back amplifies our impact.** The more we contribute—whether through teaching, mentoring, or leading—the more our knowledge and efforts continue to shape the future, even beyond our lifetime.

CONCLUSION

A Journey Begins

Talent is not just a skill-it's unique expression, a path to fulfillment, and a force for impact. Whether innate or cultivated, talent thrives through passion, perseverance, and clarity. Your journey isn't about seeking validation but about trusting your instincts and taking action.

Success is built on daily progress, resilience, and adaptability. Challenges shape growth, and setbacks are redirections, not failures. True fulfillment comes when talent aligns with purpose and its greatest power lies in sharing it with the world.

The Power of Vision and Clarity

Every great achievement begins with a well-defined dream. The stronger your emotional connection to your vision, the more likely it is to manifest. Your dreams are personal; they don't require validation from anyone else.

Clarity is crucial; exploring different paths will help you define your version of success, whether it's wealth, influence, or inner fulfillment.

Taking small, consistent steps builds momentum, reinforcing discipline and motivation over time. However, it is key to detach from immediate outcomes. Success is a process, and setbacks are often just redirections toward a better path. Your mindset shapes your reality, and what you focus on expands.

Talent as a Driving Force

True fulfillment comes from meaningful work. Talent, when cultivated, enriches life, builds confidence, and strengthens resilience. Being good at something is not enough; aligning your abilities with your career ensures long-term success.

A well-developed skill set enhances problem-solving, leadership, and adaptability, making you an asset in any field. More importantly, talent, when shared, creates a lasting impact on society.

Your childhood often holds clues to your innate strengths. Whether you play, organize, or solve puzzles, your early interests can guide you toward discovering your true potential.

Exploration is key; trying new things, observing who inspires you, and reflecting on your skills will help you uncover your unique abilities.

Creating the Right Environment for Growth

Success doesn't wait for perfect conditions; you must create them. Avoid chasing trends and instead focus on authentic self-expression. Ignore distractions, manage your energy wisely, and step outside your comfort zone to push your limits.

Planning is a skill; breaking down big goals into smaller steps makes progress more achievable. Flexibility is just as important as persistence, and tracking your progress ensures continuous improvement.

Overcoming Challenges with Resilience

Challenges are not roadblocks; they test your potential. A life without difficulties is stagnant. The key is to manage problems effectively, not turn them into suffering through overthinking. Stress reduces the quality of solutions, while a composed mind finds clarity.

Gut health also plays a surprising role in mental sharpness, energy, creativity, and motivation, which are directly linked to a well-balanced body.

Balancing Passion with Practicality

Clarity helps you navigate the balance between passion and practicality. Life presents situations; it's up to you to see them as opportunities or obstacles.

Inspired by visionaries like Elon Musk, true success requires identifying gaps, creating solutions, and executing relentlessly. Dreaming alone isn't enough—implementation is everything.

Leaving a Legacy Through Talent

Talent becomes truly meaningful when shared. Growth comes from taking responsibility for both successes and failures.

Passing on knowledge and mentoring others ensures that talent creates a ripple effect of inspiration. Great learners become great mentors, and real success is measured not just by personal achievements but by how much they contribute to others' growth.

A Call To Action

Now, it's your turn. Please take what you've learned and put it into motion. Define your dream with clarity. Take small, daily steps to build momentum.

Trust your instincts and stay true to your unique path. Challenge yourself, embrace setbacks as lessons, and never stop growing.

Share your talents with the world, inspire others, and contribute to something greater than yourself. Success isn't just about achieving—it's about becoming.

So, take action. The world is waiting for your talent to shine.

REFERENCES

https://www.ncbi.nlm.nih.gov/pmc/articles/PMC4566439/

https://mathshistory.st-andrews.ac.uk/Biographies/Ramanujan/

https://www.sciencedirect.com/science/article/abs/pii/B9780128037843000251

https://www.ncbi.nlm.nih.gov/pmc/articles/PMC3181802/

Honoré de Balzac (Author of Père Goriot) (goodreads.com)

https://www.verywellmind.com/gardners-theory-of-multiple-intelligences-2795161

https://www.ijlis.org/articles/general-study-and-importance-of-educational-and-cognitive-psychology-93242.html

https://www.simplypsychology.org/developmental-psychology.html

Kumar, A., Pramanik, J., Goyal, N., Chauhan, D., Sivamaruthi, B. S., Prajapati, B. G., & Chaiyasut, C. (2023). Gut Microbiota in Anxiety and Depression: Unveiling the Relationships and Management Options. *Pharmaceuticals*, 16(4). https://doi.org/10.3390/ph16040565

https://www.ncbi.nlm.nih.gov/pmc/articles/PMC10146621

Bull, M.J. and Plummer, N.T., 2014. Part 1: The human gut microbiome in health and disease. *Integrative Medicine: A Clinician's Journal*, 13(6), pp.17-22. Available at:

<https://www.ncbi.nlm.nih.gov/pmc/articles/PMC4566439/> [Accessed 1 Nov. 2024].

Kumar, A., Pramanik, J., Goyal, N., Chauhan, D., Sivamaruthi, B.S., Prajapati, B.G. and Chaiyasut, C., 2023. Gut microbiota in anxiety and depression: Unveiling the relationships and management options. *Pharmaceuticals*, 16(4). https://doi.org/10.3390/ph16040565

Dweck, C., 2006. Mindset: The New Psychology of Success. . https://doi.org/10.5860/choice.44-2397.

Sender, R., Fuchs, S. and Milo, R., 2016. Revised estimates for the number of human and bacteria cells in the body. *PLoS Biology*, 14(8), p.e1002533. Available at: https://pubmed.ncbi.nlm.nih.gov/27541692/ [Accessed 23 Jan. 2025].

Disclaimer

The information provided in this book is for educational and informational purposes only. The strategies, techniques, and insights shared in this book are based on research, personal experiences, and professional knowledge, but they do not guarantee specific results.

Every individual's journey of personal growth and skill mastery is unique. Success depends on multiple factors, including effort, mindset, consistency, and external circumstances. The author and publisher do not provide professional, financial, medical, or psychological advice. If you require specialized guidance, please consult a qualified professional.

While every effort has been made to ensure the accuracy and effectiveness of the content, the author and publisher assume no responsibility for any consequences resulting from the use of this book. Readers are encouraged to apply the concepts in a way that aligns with their personal goals and circumstances.

By reading this book, you acknowledge and agree that the author and publisher are not liable for any outcomes, whether positive or negative, arising from its application. Your journey of self-discovery and success is in your hands—embrace it with an open mind and a committed heart.

About The Author

Prem **Prakash Dutta** believes in living a simple yet fulfilling life guided by a spiritual mindset. With nine years of experience in the public sector banking industry, he has developed a keen eye for observing how people and society navigate challenges and find solutions in their daily lives.

A passionate traveler, Prem finds solace in exploring nature and the mountains, drawing inspiration from the beauty and wisdom of the natural world. His commitment to social causes is evident through his active participation and volunteering in awareness campaigns like **Save Soil**, working towards a better and more sustainable future.

Beyond his professional and social endeavors, Prem is deeply curious about scientific advancements. He regularly studies new research that contributes to human health and well-being. His belief that **everyone possesses unique talents**—yet only a few have become widely recognized—fuels his exploration of the nature of talent and what it takes to unlock one's true potential.

Through his writing, Prem aspires to inspire individuals to embrace their inner strengths, develop a growth-oriented mindset, and lead lives of greater purpose and fulfillment.

May I Ask You For A Small Favor?

First, I want to thank you for reading this book. You could have chosen any other book, but you took mine, and I appreciate this. I hope you have at least a few actionable insights that will positively impact your daily life.

Can I ask for 30 seconds more of your time?

I'd love it if you could leave a review of the book. That will help me grow my readership by encouraging folks to take a chance on my books.

It will take less than a minute of your time but will tremendously help me reach out to more people.

If you liked this book, please consider posting an honest review on your preferred retailer. And I'd love to see your review. Thanks for your support.